Credit Repair

How to Repair Your Credit All by Yourself

A Beginners Guide to Better Credit

By

Ernie Braveboy

INTRODUCTION

I want to thank you and congratulate you for buying the book, "Credit Repair: How to Repair Your Credit All by Yourself - A Beginners Guide to Better Credit".

Discovering that you have poor credit comes at the most inopportune of moments. Most people only find out that their credit score is bad when trying to borrow money from the bank for, say, a mortgage. Poor credit makes it very hard for the bank, or any lender for that matter, to loan you money, and even when they do, the interest rates attached are often absurdly high: it often feels as if they are trying to punish you.

As such, it is vital that you be aware of the state of your credit. If it is, as they say, "in a bad way," the thing to do is to face the problem and set out to try to fix it. Otherwise, it will come back to haunt you and you best believe it: bad credit always comes back to haunt.

This book will give you the bulk of information, tools, and knowledge you need to embark on an intensive credit repair process that will help you build a positive credit score.

Thanks again for buying this book. I hope you enjoy it!

TABLE OF CONTENTS

SECTION 1: UNDERSTANDING CREDIT & CREDIT SCORE

CHAPTER 1: UNDERSTANDING YOUR CREDIT SCORE

This chapter does not intend to analyze your particular score and give you several dozen reasons why it is what it is. This will come later and even then, we will keep it non-sensationalistic. This chapter aims to explain what credit score is; it also aims to show you what goes into a credit score.

WHAT IS YOUR CREDIT SCORE?

As you may already know, your credit score is a 3-digit number generated from information that appears in your credit score, by a mathematical algorithm. Above all other things, a credit score is, by design, supposed to "predict risk."

You see, the bank or lender has no way of truly knowing if a borrower is honest and prompt in repaying back loaned amounts except by going by his or her credit score. Your credit score shows the bank or any other lender just how high the probability of not honoring credit obligations is, in the 24 months or so after the generation of your score. Going by this, it is clear that the primary use of the credit score is to "define you" to the bank or lender.

As far as the credit score goes, there are multiple scoring models available. Of them all, the FICO credit score is the dominant model. Whether you choose to take them at their word or not, www.myFICO.com claim that well over 90% of all US institutions employ FICO scores as they try and make financial decisions.

WHAT IS THE FICO SCORE RANGE?

The FICO score ranges from 300 to 850, with 300 being the base score and 850 being the highest possible score. A higher number is indicative of lower risk.

As a consumer, you will have 3 FICO scores. Each FICO score will come in each of the three credit reports that you have a right to. The three major bureaus: Transunion, Experian, and Equifax provide these credit reports.

NOTE: Unfortunately, today, you can only access FICO scores on both Equifax and Transunion. Experian ended its agreement with FICO in 2009. However, other credit score models will be included in the Experian report).

WHAT GOES INTO YOUR CREDIT SCORE?

The data from the credit report will go into five major categories that will make up the FICO score.

Naturally, the model will consider some factors more significant, factors such as a debt owed and payment history. Here are the categories:⌐

1: PAYMENT HISTORY (35%)

This shows payment information on your account.

2: AMOUNTS OWED (30%)

This points to how much you owe. The credit amount available and in use is heavily weighted.

3: LENGTH OF CREDIT HISTORY (15%)

This points to how long ago you opened your accounts as well as time since account activity.

4: CREDIT TYPE USED (10%)

This is the "accounts mix" you have. There are varied account types such as installment and revolving.

5: NEW CREDIT (10%)

This is the pursuit of new credit. This is inclusive of credit inquiries as well as the total number of newly opened accounts.

NOTE: Chapter 4 will have a proper evaluation of each of these five categories.

CHAPTER 2: UNDERSTANDING CREDIT REPORTS

What is a credit report and how often should you expect one? What can you expect to see your credit reports?☐

In the most simplistic of terms, a credit report is a "compilation of information" regarding the way you go about handling debt. It includes information on how much debt you have managed to accrue, how you go about paying your bills (are you always on time or behind?), where you work, where you go home to, if you have ever filed for bankruptcy, and whether your vehicle has ever been repossessed or your house foreclosed.

Does it look as though the credit report has too much information? Well, if it looks that way, it is because it actually does.

HOW DOES INFORMATION GET ON THE CREDIT REPORT?

TIP: Credit bureaus are the ones that (usually) maintain credit reports. Credit bureaus, or credit reporting agencies, are businesses that specialize in credit management.

The previous chapter mentioned the three major credit bureaus in the US: Equifax, Experian, and Transunion. Corporations that do business with you have an agreement with the credit bureaus to send information to them (or at the very least, to send information to one of them.) These bureaus will then update the information they receive on your credit report. Most of your loan accounts and credit cards are updated on the credit report on a monthly basis.

Regarding the last sentence of the previous paragraph, this is not always the case with all businesses. Not all businesses will update the bureaus on your financial information on a monthly basis. However, the bulk of these businesses will indeed get in touch with the bureaus once you do not make your payments.

Here is an example: your cable bill will usually not be included in your credit report. However, if you do fall 6 months behind in payments, you can expect the cable company to tell on you, and the cable bill to appear on your credit report.

WHAT TYPE OF INFORMATION IS INCLUDED IN THE CREDIT REPORT?

This is a mere overview to help you understand what your credit report really is; a more detailed evaluation of this will be available in the next chapter.

A credit report is a lot like an over glorified identity card in that it contains your basic identity information: your name, home address, place of employment, etc.

You must understand that your credit report may not always be perfect. There may be mistakes such as misspellings of your name as well as inaccurate addresses and employers. At times, this is because of mistakes made by the business that forwarded your information. At other times, this may be because of identity theft.

As such, it is very important that you go through all your credit reports with a fine toothcomb. It could be that your credit is suffering through no fault of your own, and you are atoning for someone else's financial sins.

CHECKING YOUR CREDIT REPORT

It is important that you order your credit report at least once a year as a way to ensure that the information on it is correct. If you are trying to repair your credit, it is wise to order it with more frequency. The same applies to a case where you are gearing to apply for a major loan. If you suspect you are a victim of identity theft, insist on frequent credit reports and then report any mishaps that recur to these bureaus.

NOTE: You have a right to one free credit report from all three credit bureaus every year. Chapter 6 also shows you how you can access these credit reports.

WHAT CAN YOU EXPECT TO SEE ON YOUR CREDIT REPORT?

As this very chapter has indicated, a credit report will have basic personal details such as your name, your date of birth, your address, and the likes. As we said in an earlier part of this chapter, it is of utmost importance that you perform a thorough evaluation of the information contained in your credit report to ensure it is accurate. Note, however, that past addresses appearing on your credit report are not a bad thing. Here are other elements you can expect to see on your credit report:

1. Your credit report will also list any financial issues of the legal kind that you may have had. Here, we are talking the likes of liens, wage garnishment, judgment, and bankruptcy. If you have any of these elements on your credit score, understand that they may be a major reason why your credit score is so poor. However, take

comfort in the fact that these elements will not dictate the state of your credit forever; they should not have to anyway. At the very least, even if you are passive in trying to repair them, they will inevitably age off.

2. Your credit report will also contain creditor information. In fact, this is what will make up the bulk of your credit report. This is inclusive of different accounts that you have (think credit cards, loans, and the like), their present status (closed, opened, in collections, etc.), credit limits, balances, as well as details on payment frequency. Of course, if you have some missed payments, you can mostly expect them to show up and to contribute to the overall weight of your score. The same applies for late payments. It is from all these details that your credit score is generated.

I believe that you now understand what makes up your credit report as well as your credit score. The next logical step is to understand what makes an excellent or poor credit score.

The next chapter covers this in detail.

CHAPTER 3: WHAT MAKES A CREDIT SCORE EXCELLENT OR POOR

Your credit score is somewhat like a disciplinary record as far as finance and credit management goes. The lower your credit score, the more likely it is that you are not great at managing your finances and as such, you are an unnecessary risk, at least as far as getting a loan goes.

A person with a high credit score, on the other hand, is an attractive individual to banks and lenders: he or she can ask for any amount desired, and the bank or lender is likely to give it whilst keeping interest rates favorable (usually).

Think about it this way: a fellow with a high credit score could decide to take up a loan tomorrow, be it to finance a new car or a new house, and he or she would be confident of getting it. To them, it is a matter of WHEN they can access the loan. If you, on the other hand, have a less than desirable credit score, it really is a matter of IF you can get the loan. As such, your credit score is something you should take very seriously.

This chapter will revisit the factors introduced in Chapter 1 and add flesh to them for they are the factors that carry all the weight with regard to the state of your credit score.

FACTOR #1: PAYMENT HISTORY

This will account for the biggest slice of your credit score. Just how well do you pay off your bills every month? Given that a whopping 35% of the credit score relies on this one, it may be time to take monthly bills more seriously.

Under every loan you have ever taken, under every credit card or mortgage you have ever had, you will be able to see on your credit report, how much money you have paid towards it for a stretch of time, in comparison to the total monthly period of the particular loan. If the monthly bill totals $551 and you barely ever pay over $300 towards this bill in a month, this will tell a story that will be all too apparent, going by your credit score.

Other creditors will rarely bother to update the bureaus monthly but will do so once the payments fall behind by several months. Such companies include utility companies, cell phone companies, and cable services.

If there are late payments on the credit report, there will be information on just how late these payments were. The later the payment is, the more you can expect the credit score to fall.

FACTOR #2: YOUR TOTAL DEBT

30% of your FICO score will be relative to how much debt you have accrued. Installment loans such as student loans and mortgages will not weigh quite as heavily as, for example, your revolving debt.

Your revolving debt is inclusive of your credit cards. Lenders tend to keep a keen eye on your debt-to-credit ratio. They like to call it "credit utilization." Your debt-to-credit-ratio, or credit utilization, calculate just how much you owe in comparison to the maximum credit line present in your credit cards.

If you are close to maxing out a card you own, you can bet that your credit score suffers as a result. Here is the thing, however—we are speaking ratios here. Two fellows can owe the same debt on their card but end up having a very wide difference, with regard to their credit scores, if their maximum balances differ.

Here is an example:

A person with $3,000 debt on his credit card, with a $10,000 maximum balance only has 30% credit utilization. Another person with a similar $3,000 credit card charged amount but with a halved credit card limit of $5,000 is walking around with a 60%

ratio. Assuming all other things are equal, the $5,000 credit limit fellow will have a much lower score.

FACTOR #3: CREDIT HISTORY LENGTH

This will account for 15% of your credit score. This is because a lender cannot possibly gauge your willingness, or ability, to repay loans if you do not have some sort of record proving that you can be able to do so. The scoring model will take into account just how long various accounts you own have been open, inclusive of credit cards and loans.

Here is some mood-dampening news. Rent payments are never part of the FICO score (If they were, the absolute top tip, with regard to repairing your credit, would have a lot to do with having your rental payments reflect on your credit report. But then again, your credit would likely not be bad.)

FACTOR #4: NEW CREDIT

When you read your credit report, you will see a section called "inquiries." "Inquiries" simply refers to every credit application you have submitted over the last 24 months. This can affect up to 10% of your overall score.

Each inquiry present will take off 5 or so points from your score during the 1st year. The exception will be if you completed multiple inquiries within a few weeks. If this is your situation, then it is merely indicative that you went out for some rate shopping for a credit card or loan. That batch of inquiries, thus, will be treated as just one inquiry.

FACTOR #5: CREDIT MIX

This will contribute to the final 10% of your score. The types of credit you have will contribute to how high your score is. In this very chapter, we mention that revolving debt, inclusive of credit cards, will heavily influence your credit score when compared to installment loans. Installment loans will usually have some asset or other tied to them, such as a car or a house.

One major reason why installment loans will have less of a negative influence on your credit score is that they signal that you have some asset of value that you are naturally committed to paying for, so you can continue to own it. It is very hard to say the same for purchases you make on impulse, on your credit card, which is why the penalty is higher for these.

Student loans have a favorable outlook primarily because they signal an investment into future earning power. In truth, the lender is a very simple entity, with a proclivity toward thinking linearly. The lender will say, *"If this guy took out this student loan to pay for his law degree, then he will be able to make more money in a few years. The more money this guy makes, the faster he will be able to pay off his loans. Even more importantly, the more money this guy makes, the more he will be able to put himself in a position to borrow more from us, which means more profits."*

If you can monitor and manage these factors well, you can build a positive credit score even if yours is in bad shape right now. Later chapters of this guide will show you how to repair a bad credit score.

In the next chapter, we will discuss why you should repair your credit score (in other words, the implications of having a bad credit score)

CHAPTER 4: WHY REPAIR POOR CREDIT

You probably have more than a few ideas why it is important to repair poor credit. Regardless, this chapter is a necessary read all the same.

There are so many reasons why it is necessary to maintain a healthy credit score—that is beside the obvious one of being able to walk to the bank and being eligible for a loan.

Let us examine some reasons why you must maintain healthy credit.

#1: YOU SAVE A LOT OF MONEY ON INTEREST

You already know this one, but here it is anyway: *a low credit score only prompts the lender to raise the interest charged.*

The lower your credit score, the higher you can expect the interest charged on loans to be, and this is if you are lucky enough to convince the lender that you are a worthy prospect of a loan.

Once you repair your credit, you will immediately enjoy competitive interest rates. Do you know why lenders will suggest absurdly high-interest rates and believe they can get away with it? Because not only does your poor credit show that you are untrustworthy, the lender knows that your lending options are severely limited because of your less than desirable credit.

#2: YOU WILL NOT HAVE TO PAY HIGH-SECURITY DEPOSITS

Utility service companies—even phone companies—like to check a person's credit score before allowing the said person to establish service. If the score is poor, these service providers charge a deposit to, in their words, "offset the risk of default." Only when you make your payments on time will you be able to get back your deposit.

#3: YOU WILL BE ABLE TO GET A LOWER INSURANCE RATE

This is not something we made up for this book: the state of your credit determines your insurance premiums. This includes all sorts of insurances: life, auto, home, and the likes. Simply put, a bad credit history will mean paying more for insurance than you otherwise would with healthy credit in place.

#4: YOU WILL NOT BE COMPELLED TO PAY WITH CASH FOR JUST ABOUT EVERYTHING

Bad credit makes it difficult to get credit cards. This will mean having to walk around with cash everywhere. This will likely not be something that puts you off… until you need to do something like rent a car. Renting a car will require you to pay an extra deposit amount if you do not pay using a credit card.

#5: You Will Be Eligible For A Higher Credit Limit

Once you show that you can pay your bills on time—the creditor will be very eager to increase your credit limit. However, your creditor will still check your credit score just to be sure that you are truly deserving of an increased credit limit. Here is when things start to get interesting: if your credit score is outright poor, the creditor may actually decide that, rather than being deserving of a credit limit increase, your credit limit actually needs slashing.

SECTION 2: NEGATIVE ITEMS ON THE CREDIT REPORT

CHAPTER 5: EVALUATING NEGATIVE ITEMS THAT MAY APPEAR ON YOUR CREDIT REPORT

Before we go on ahead and examine negative items on your credit report, here are a few things to understand:

1. The FCRA limits the time length that a credit bureau may report negative items on the credit report. The same bureau(s) will often report positive as well as neutral items indefinitely.

2. The extent to which every negative item hurts your credit score will fade gradually, albeit slowly, with time. The lesson here is that unless you go ahead and ignore this book's call to implement positive credit behavior, it is impossible to have bad credit forever.

3. Negative items do not have to sit and stew for years until time peels them off. It is very possible to remove negative items from your credit report much earlier than their expiry date. However, this is not always possible and always depends on your unique situation, and if your request to have them taken off is acceptable to the creditor. Still, if you write to the bureaus and ask nicely, the probability of them taking the blemish off your credit report tends to be high,

especially since so very few people bother to write and ask. But then again, not many people go out of their way to read positive, actionable credit repair material as you are doing right now.

4. The smart man or woman is far more aggressive with the removal of more recent negative items than with the older ones. The logic behind this is simple enough: the older the negative item is, the sooner it will age out and fall off your annual credit report. Newer negative items will be around for long. Unless the older negative item is truly hurting any chances of getting a higher credit score, focus the bulk of your energy towards "prematurely" removing newer negative items.

With all of this said, let us look at the types of negative items you may find on your credit report. You will also discover how long you can expect these items to sit around if you do not go out of your way to have them removed early:

ITEM #1: CHARGE-OFFS

A charge off will occur when the creditor makes the decision that they may not be able to collect your debt. Instead of having the debt on their books and have it registered as debt that is past its due date, the creditor decides to eliminate the debt from past due accounts in their books.

It does not end there, however. By having the debt charged off, the company sees its accounts receivable report automatically improve. Still, this does not mean that the debt is cleared off and has disappeared. In a majority of cases, the debt will be sold to a debt buyer (yes, debt buyers exist), who will pay the company and then go right ahead and expect that you pay the full amount owed.

The debt buyer will insist that you pay the full amount owed, inclusive of the likes of court fees, late charges, interest, etc. The debt buyer will more or less make sure that they miss nothing.

You may be asking yourself what court fees have to do with any of this. Well, these debt buyers prefer to collect by contacting you and immediately taking you to court so they can collect the full value of the debt and applicable fees that arise. A charge off is not a desirable thing to have hanging over your credit.☐

A charge off can sit and stew on your credit report for up to 7 years and a further 180 days.

ITEM #2: COLLECTIONS

Collections tend to be tricky things because paying them off could actually inflict more damage to your credit score as the starting date of when the collection was reported may be reset.

Never jump straight into paying off a collection: read all the paperwork available until you understand everything. Use the services of a lawyer if you have to, but make sure that you go through everything carefully and understand how every available course of action will affect your credit.

Just like a charge off and if unaddressed, a collection will hover for 7 years from the day that you first fell behind.

ITEM #3: LATE PAYMENTS

It will not matter if you actually catch up on the amounts you owe. Any payment that you fall behind paying for 30 days can appear on your credit report. The positive news here is that many creditors tend to hold off reporting a late payment until you get too comfortable and have a 2nd late payment. You see, they do not want to upset good customers, also known as biting the hand that feeds them.

Lenders can report late payments for up to 7 years.

ITEM #4: BANKRUPTCIES

Bankruptcies will be reported for "no more than 10 years" from the filing date, which in itself, despite its sympathetic nature, is not a line that will make most people smile. 10 years is a long time to have your credit dragged down by a negative item. If your case is dismissed, then the countdown begins from the date of dismissal.

ITEM #5: FORECLOSURES

A foreclosure may be reported for up to 7 years. However, this one tends to be very easy to walk around. Once you get your financial balance back, you could always go on and buy a new house, as well as seek to have the foreclosure removed by writing to the bureaus.

ITEM #6: JUDGMENTS

These may appear for up to 7 years from the filing date of the lawsuit or until the governing limitations statute expires—whichever hangs around for longer. Most limitation statutes tend to expire sooner than 7 years, and as such, we are talking about 7 years as a maximum.

ITEM #7: REPOSSESSIONS

These may be reported for up to 7 years.

ITEM #8: TAX LIENS

The taxman is brutal here, seeing as, under federal law, tax liens that go unpaid may be reported indefinitely. However, credit bureaus often decide

10 years is long enough to have these appear and subsequently remove them after a decade.☐

Now that we have the basics out of the way, the chapters from this one onwards will show you how to overhaul your credit score. To do so, the first thing you need to do is give your credit report, once you have it, a thorough evaluation.

ERNIE BRAVEBOY

SECTION 3: OVERHAULING YOUR CREDIT STATE

CHAPTER 6: STEP 1 – THOROUGHLY EVALUATE EACH CREDIT REPORT

Well, we are somewhat putting the cart before the horse here. Before making a thorough evaluation of the credit reports, naturally, the first thing you need to do is to access them.

As this book has said, there are 3 credit bureaus—Experian, Transunion, and Equifax—and you have a right to at least one credit report from each of these bureaus yearly.

Assuming you have not accessed your credit reports or you have had some trouble trying to access them, here is how you can access your free report:

1. Go to www.AnnualCreditReport.com

2. The interface is simple and direct: enter the personal information requested. You will have to answer a few security-related questions, which is necessary because it guards against malicious identity thieves.

3. After verifying your identity, the portal will redirect you to a page where you will be able to download all credit reports from the 3 bureaus. It should not take too long to download them—unless you have a slow internet connection.

4. If you are an old-fashioned person who likes to have hardcopy versions along with the softcopy ones, you can call 1-877-322-8228, verify your identity to the consumer care personality at the end of the line, and request hard copies of your credit reports mailed to your address.

With this out of the way, let us look at thoroughly evaluating each credit report:

THOROUGHLY EVALUATING EACH CREDIT REPORT: HOW TO

Once you have accessed your credit reports, the next logical step is to go over them with a fine toothcomb and check them for accuracy. The 3 credit reports will not necessarily be the same because some creditors only bother to report to one or two of the three bureaus. Thus, having one item appearing in one or two reports, but missing from the third one, does not outright mean reporting mistakes.

Still, you should carefully check and determine the accuracy of the reporting. A creditor may only report to two out of three bureaus, but the information appears differently on both reports. The creditor could report to all 3 bureaus but the information is only similar in two out of the three credit reports.

Never assume that the information is similar across all 3 reports. Check to make sure it is.

Here is a simplistic guide on how to evaluate your credit reports thoroughly:

1. The first step is to make sure that basic personal information is recorded correctly. Ensure that there are no other persons listed on your credit report. Only after doing this should you proceed to the rest of the points here.

2. Take note of any section that appears incorrectly reported, from the account opening date to highest balance had. Be especially thorough on negative items, such as reported late payments. Make sure that you indeed own all credit lines.

3. Focus more on the report's negative report section and ensure everything is accurate. You will find all accounts that you have not paid as per agreement, public records you have had, collections, etc. This is your credit's "hurt factory": everything that shows up here is responsible for the bulk of the damage to your credit score.☐

Once you have thoroughly analyzed your credit report, the other thing you need to do is:

CHAPTER 7: STEP 2 – PINPOINT THE CREDIT SCORE KILLERS

This chapter picks up from where the previous chapter finished. Once you have gone through your credit reports and especially gone through the negative items sections, you have some idea of the elements that are hurting your credit score.

The next step is to dig deeper and determine which items are truly hurting your credit. Doing this is not hard and is, in fact, something you can easily do yourself. □

As previously covered in this book, there are only 5 score factors that determine your credit score. As we have covered as well, these factors do not carry equal weight.

1. Start by examining payment history such as late payments on your report. Again, it is important to know that your payment history will be the most vital factor. 35% of your score will hinge on this. Even a singular late payment will significantly drag down your credit score. If you have several late payments on your report, they are very likely the reason why your credit is doing so badly.

2. The next area to look at is credit utilization, which determines 30% of your credit score. This is inclusive of revolving credit (covered previously in this book, revolving credit points to the likes of credit cards and home equity credit lines). Your credit utilization also referred to as credit to debt ratio, shows lenders just how responsible you are with your finances. If your credit limit is $10,000 and you owe $9,500 on the credit card, it does not take a genius to figure out why your credit score looks bad.

3. Credit account age plays a serious role in credit score generation, which is why it is bizarre that so many people frequently ditch old credit cards in favor of new ones. An older set of credit cards is an asset, going by age alone, and your credit score will be higher because of it. 15% of your credit score will hinge on this. If your youthful credit account age is the major reason your credit score is poor, the only repair measure is to sit on your lily pad and wait for them to age some more.

4. Do you have a healthy mix of credit accounts? Having a varied mix of accounts, or lack of one, will play a part in determining how high your score is. There are two main credit types: revolving accounts (think in the lines of credit and credit cards) and installment accounts (think

student loans, mortgages, car loans, etc.). A creditor likes to see that you can competently handle both credit types.

5. Your credit application history also counts when it comes to your credit score. If you have applied for multiple credit accounts of late, it may explain why your score is less than desirable. 10% of your credit score hinges on this particular subject. This one will take quite some time to fix, but the good news is that the longer you go without accumulating extra credit accounts, the lesser the impact on your score will be.

Once you go through all these factors on your report, you will find out soon enough what is damaging your credit score. What do you do next? One of the fastest ways to see true credit improvement is to fix any errors appearing on your credit report, which is what the next chapter covers.

CHAPTER 8: STEP 3 – CLEAN UP THE CREDIT REPORTS

The way to go about cleaning up errors on your credit report is by disputing these errors. You will want to begin your dispute process as soon as you can if you want to see quick improvement on your credit.

Speaking of disputes, you can go about repairing credit on your own, which is actionable enough, or you can use the services of a credit repair professional, which will certainly cost you money but end up worth it in the end. Whatever you choose to do, it is vital that you begin disputing immediately.

Here is a link to a detailed guide showing how to carry out a dispute process:

https://www.credit.com/credit-repair/credit-repair-content/dispute-credit-report-error/

This book will focus on spotting errors and acting with speed to dispute them; however, other than misspellings and outright false information on the credit report, what do you look for when determining what account to dispute? Here are a few red flags:

1. The information is inaccurate. It could be that descriptive details are laid out all wrong, the amounts owed are wrong, or a late payment is still recorded as outstanding even though you have already paid it.

2. The information is untimely. Look out for dates inaccurately recorded. Dates fed all wrong may not mean much to you, but they may definitely mean a lot to a creditor down the line. Besides, why should you accept inaccurately recorded information on something as vital as your credit report?

3. The information is biased. This one is often rare thanks to the staccato, professional nature of credit reports. Nevertheless, do not rule it out altogether.

4. The information is incomplete. It could be that some information is in the record without including the whole package in so that ultimately, it reflects badly on you and by extension, your credit score.

5. The information is questionable. Do you believe that there is information that you can question? Do you feel that some of the things recorded do not reflect your financial activities accurately? Identity theft is a thing that you should be on the lookout for.

NOTE: It is your right as well as the responsibility for an error-free credit report. The nice person act has to make way for necessary action no matter how much you feel like you are being a nuisance to the folks at the bureau. You are obligated to an accurate credit report. Be aggressive and thorough in your attempts to clean up your credit report.

HOW DIFFICULT IS THE DISPUTE PROCESS?

The answer is simple: it is not. Many people do not realize that while they sit passively, believing the dispute procedure to be too much work, there are thousands of U.S. citizens successfully disputing dubious information on their credit reports every day.

Still, even 10,000 people disputing errors in their credit reports are only a small percentage of Americans. Too many people sabotage their financial health by refusing to dispute unfair errors.

How do you dispute?

Here is a simplistic guide to carrying out a successful dispute:

1. Mail a certified letter to the credit bureau. There is a link in this chapter to a dispute letter guide. Make sure you clearly outline the negative item(s).

2. Make sure you keep a copy of the letter. The credit bureau will undoubtedly get back to you within the month but in case they do not, you could always sue them, and use your letter copy as evidence of their negligence.

3. Disputing your errors online is a bit of a waste of time. There are those who swear by it but it is an open secret that you will get better and quicker results when you bother to write and mail a dispute letter.

4. Detail all the incorrect information in the letter. If you have documents that support your claim, attach copies.

5. Include, clearly and correctly so, all your basic personal information such as your name and address.

6. Use a professional tone all through. It is vital that the bureau takes you seriously. Ranting will only make you seem like a bit of a joke.

7. Once you dispute, the law requires prompt investigation. The law compels the creditor to produce proof of his claim's accuracy.

8. Remember, you may have to go back and forth a few times with the credit bureaus. However, if you keep at it, they will eventually crack.

Once you dispute an error, the credit-reporting agency or bureau has to respond to your claim in the space of one month (30 days) as obligated by law. Thus, you do not have to fear to have to wait indefinitely, and your credit doing badly all along.☐

Here are additional tips that will help you as you seek to dispute errors in your credit report(s). You may have to write more than one letter as you attempt to have errors cleared from your report:

1. Dispute each mistake with each bureau. Some people believe that disputing a mistake that recurs on all 3 credit reports with one bureau will fix everything. If you do this, the likeliest result is that one credit report will come up clean while the others will still carry the errors.

2. It is common to find more than one error in a credit report. Attempting to dispute all the errors that appear in a wholesale fashion where you lump everything in one dispute letter and send it to the bureaus is a good way to send a message that your dispute does not need seriousness. It is paramount that you dispute each account separately.

3. There is an exception to the above point. If you see several mistakes on one account, it is all right to group the entire pile of mistakes into a single dispute.

4. It is very possible to dispute errors without necessarily using the services of an expert and indeed, many people have done it and achieved success. However, it may be confusing, especially when errors appear sporadically in different credit reports. A reputable credit repair corporation or a lawyer will charge you a fee, but you can guarantee that the job will be thorough.

5. Speaking of credit repair companies, the company that promises you an outright 300-point leap in your score is selling you a pile of nonsense. In fact, even if this was somehow possible, the truth is that it would be almost impossible to accomplish without illegal, Black Hand tactics.

Here is a link showing what a sample repair letter looks like:

https://www.credit.com/credit-repair/credit-repair-letters/

After this, the next step is to:

CHAPTER 9: STEP 4 – EVALUATE ACCOUNTS IN COLLECTIONS & CONTINUE CLOSELY MONITORING YOUR CREDIT

These are two distinct aspects of repairing your credit scores and therefore, we will look at them individually:

HOW TO EVALUATE ACCOUNTS IN COLLECTIONS

Take a closer look at your recent collections. Payment history has the biggest impact on your credit score—at least looking at the 35% influence accompanying it. However, the credit score of most Americans suffers mostly because of the state of their collections.

Recent collections inflict the most damage to the average American's credit score seeing as the penalization of newer debt is significantly heavier when coming up with a credit score. It is also important to pay attention to the debt type you are carrying and paying off.

Here are a few gems of debt and paying it off:□

1. Medical debts tend not to affect your credit score with the same viciousness as other debt

kinds do. Thus, do not make medical debt your first object of focus.

2. When making a debt payment, if you can, make full payments. There is no crime in making partial payments, but partial payments may only reset the time limit, with regard to how long the accounts remain in your report, which may have a bad influence on your score for a longer time.

3. Too many people refuse to consider settlements as a way of getting financially freer and fixing their credit. Attempt to negotiate a settlement with the collection agency. A negotiation settlement will see you pay less than the amounts you owe. If there ever was a downside to doing this, it is that you may have to report the exact amount dismissed as income. Doing this on your tax return information could well result in heavier taxes. You could even go up a higher income bracket, meaning you will be subject to a higher tax rate.

4. On occasion, a collection agency will pretend to be blind to your efforts to pay off debt and will go on acting as though you have made no effort to pay off debt. To avoid such frauds, make sure all payment agreements are in writing and that you have copies. It will be very hard for the

collection agency to dismiss your claims in court when you have written documents.

CONTINUE MONITORING YOUR CREDIT SCORE

You have taken care of accounts in collections. Make sure that the changes you have made find their way onto your credit report. It is certainly too ambitious to expect the changes to appear next week, but within a couple of months, maximum, the accounts should have dropped off.

Wait at least 8 weeks, check your credit report again, and raise the issue with the credit bureau if you find nothing has changed. How do you do this? You follow the information in the previous chapter on disputing your credit report.

The next step now is to take a proactive approach to repairing your credit score. The next chapter/step talks about how to so this

CHAPTER 10: STEP 5 – START A POSITIVE CREDIT HISTORY

Beyond disputing errors and staying away from irresponsible financial behavior that reflects badly on your credit score, one of the most potent ways to fix your credit is to go on and start to build a positive credit history.

We call it positive history because the actions you take today will indeed be history a few months or years from now. It could be that a lender has denied you credit today, but this does not mean complete borrowing prohibition.

This brings us to this vital point with regard to building a positive credit history. If your credit utilization, payment history, or account mix are all keeping you away from a good credit score, it is a good strategy to open new credit, which may help you build up your credit at a faster rate. Enter the secured credit card…

THE SECURED CREDIT CARD

We will describe the secured credit card as "a card meant to help you" and indeed, secured credit cards are powerful tools when it comes to building your credit.

The secured card requires you to pitch in a deposit amount. This deposit amount will double up and serve as your credit limit. If you are late in paying your bills, the card company may dip into your deposit for the amounts owed.

Still, the point of opening this kind of card, as well as doing all other activities to improve your credit, is to combine them with responsible financial behavior: pay your bills on time and make sure your credit utilization speaks well of you. A person with a $1,000 deposit, which means a $1,000 credit limit on the secured card, is making no headway at all if he/she goes ahead and charges $800 from said card.

BENEFITS OF A SECURED CREDIT CARD

Depending on where you are, with regard to your financial and credit state, a secured card could see you make significant credit headway in as little as 6 months. Well, you could see changes within a month, but the key word here is "significant." Here are some benefits that come with a secured card:

1. The secured credit card presents a way to obtain higher credit scores even when unpleasant negative items remain in your report. You may be unapproved for a traditional credit card but most of the time, still be eligible for a secured

credit card as they present less risk for the creditor.

2. Moreover, your card issuer will make a point of reporting to the bureaus that you are a fellow with the ability to pay the card on time, which will reflect well on your score.

3. If you were to default on your payment, the security deposit on your card will be the one used. Using the security deposit will mean that even though you default, the card will still be paid, seeing as your funds "secure it." This phenomenon is why we refer to it as a secured credit card.

With the 5 steps we have discussed in the last few chapters, your credit repair journey should be well on its way, full steam ahead. The next chapter has some essential tips and a few fast tried & tested tips that will boost your credit in a short time span

SECTION 4: TRIED & TESTED TIPS THAT WILL BOOST YOUR CREDIT SCORE FAST

CHAPTER 11: QUICK STRATEGIES YOU CAN IMPLEMENT TO GIVE YOUR CREDIT A NEW LOOK IN A SHORT TIME

Having negative items struck out of your credit report may see your credit score improve rapidly. However, having a negative item removed will usually take a lot of time. Still, even as you follow the directives of this chapter, it is important that you do your best to have negative items removed. Having said that, let us move on…

Suppose you are looking for quick developments, with regard to your credit score getting healthier. Suppose you only have a couple of months to bump up your credit score. This chapter will show you several fixes that will greatly influence your credit score in a short space of time:

FIX #1: LOWER THE CREDIT UTILIZATION RATIO

This book has more than adequately covered credit utilization. The closer you are to maxing out your cards, the more unfortunate the state of your credit will be and the lower the credit score shall be.

How do you lower your credit utilization ratio? You do it by paying down credit card balances. Begin with maxed out cards, or close to it, as this is where the real rot is. Clearing out several maxed out cards could see you attain a 100-point score jump, which is not a small thing.

FIX #2: REQUEST AN INCREASE IN YOUR CREDIT CARD LIMITS

What happens if you are in no position to pay off multiple debts on your multiple credit cards? There is still a chance of making score improvements. The thing to do is to pick up your phone and request one, or several of your credit card companies, to increase your credit card limit.

It is not in your interest to charge a higher amount than you owe already. All you want is to have a higher credit card limit. In case you have not drawn a conclusion yet, a higher credit limit will mean that the balance you owe takes up a smaller percentage of available credit. In other words, the result is a better credit utilization ratio.

Here is an example.

Assume you owe $5,000 on a credit card that has a $10,000 limit. As it stands, your credit utilization is at 50%, which is not too impressive to the lender, and the algorithm that spits out your credit score. However, if you can have your credit limit bumped up to $15,000; your credit utilization will immediately drop to 35%, assuming you do not go ahead and charge more on the same card.

It will help to have a positive payment history when you make the call. The card company will be more inclined to hear you out if you have a record of making payments on time.

FIX #3: BECOME AN AUTHORIZED USER

It is a shame that more people do not use this tactic despite its immense effectiveness and requires almost total passiveness from your part. To implement it, find a close relative or friend. Make sure that this character has a strong, long-standing credit and proceed to ask him or her if you can become an authorized user on an account or two that they own. The account will promptly become part of your report… in its entirety. If the person's credit is truly strong, you could see as much as a 100-point score increase in a matter of weeks, all from doing little more than ask.

Of course, there are more than a few risks involved with this one. Your friend could decide to go over to the dark side and refuse to make payments, or consistently start making late payments. Your friend could also be carrying a large balance on his account. The goodwill appears hand in hand with the bad, and you can expect to see it all laid out on your credit report. The tactic, simply put, requires caution.

FIX #4: CONSOLIDATE CREDIT CARD DEBT

Another potent way to repair your credit score fast is to consider a debt consolidation loan. This one is somewhat like fighting fire with fire, but it actually works. This sort of loan is a personal loan type that you will channel toward paying off the various credit cards in your possession. You then pay a singular monthly balance on this personal loan.

You may be able to save some good money by getting a lower interest rate on the loan (this will require that you negotiate with the lender), but this will be dependent on the interest rates on your credit cards. If they are not too high, then you stand a good chance.

Still, even if the credit card interest rates are through the roof, it is possible to find a lender who will still slash off the loan rate anyway. Arm yourself with a preapproval and shop around for the best rates. As far as the monthly payments on this sort of loan go, you could break even, and your credit score would still see a marked increase. This is because this loan falls into the installment loan category, a category viewed more favorably.

FIX #5: CONSIDER GETTING A CREDIT BUILDING LOAN

You will have to approach smaller banks, or banks steeped away from the traditional bank format. Smaller banks, even credit unions, offer credit builder loans to individuals who want to fix their credit issues.

Once you take out the loan, the lender will deposit the money into a secured account. So secured is this account that in fact, you will not be able to access it. You will then proceed with making payments toward the loan on a monthly basis. Only when you repay the entire loan will the lender releases the funds so you can use them. It is a lot like unlocking levels on a video game.

Making payments on monies you cannot spend seems a bit bizarre. Still, it makes sense: the bank has to protect itself, and this move offers you a proper chance to prove that you can be a responsible adult as far as the issue of borrowed money goes.

Even better, once you complete making the payments, the bank will go ahead and report to the credit bureaus that you are a borrower who is able to pay his dues on time. This will have a positive effect on your credit score.

SECTION 5: WHAT TO EXPECT (AND WHAT NEXT) AFTER FIXING YOUR CREDIT SCORE

CHAPTER 12: HOW LONG IT TAKES TO OVERHAUL YOUR CREDIT SCORE

With the right strategies—such as those contained in the previous chapter—and an aggressive, determined mindset, you could go a long way toward improving your score in 30 days. You could even be able to improve your score by 100+ points, which is quite phenomenal.

It is true that you can make significant headway in a month. However, how long will it take to really turn your credit around and have it at an excellent state? How long will it take you to fix your credit completely so that the unpleasant items disappear completely? From a realistic standpoint, how long will a complete overhaul take?

The answer to the questions is certainly not 30 days. Even a couple of years would be ambitious unless you either had very few negative items in place or somehow successfully applied to have every negative item on your credit report removed.

Credit revisions usually take time. Some people think that if you dispute everything on your credit report, you will somehow compel the bureaus to revise your credit. However, it is pointless to dispute accurate information on your report. If you indeed made 3 late payments in the last financial year and your creditor reported this, all a dispute will do is waste your time, the bureau's time, and that of the creditor—and the negative item will still reappear next time.

THE 7 YEAR LIMIT

Typically, most negative items take 7 years to age off and fall off your report with the exceptions being bankruptcies and unpaid tax liens that often hang around for at least a decade.

With this said, you do not have to sit passively and wait for the negative items to fall off. One great strategy to have the negative items removed, especially if you have since paid off the outstanding amounts, is to write to your creditor and request to have the item removed. It is true that a mere request may get you your desired revision (they call it goodwill), but it is likelier that you will have to settle for some financial settlement or other, in order for them to remove the negative item. Nevertheless, expect the process to take some time, since your creditor may insist on checking your recent financial record to determine if you deserve having the item taken off your report.

STEADY IMPROVEMENTS SHOULD CONTRIBUTE TO THE BIGGER PICTURE

With all of this said, while you may have to wait several years to see a total overhaul of your credit situation, you could see significant, marked improvements every few weeks, especially if you combine the credit repair strategies covered in the previous chapter with responsible credit handling.

Here is a strategy that will help keep your credit score improvement consistent. Since the typical American is obsessed with his or her credit card, ensure you keep your credit utilization at 30% or below. Let us now look at how to ensure that your credit health remains great.

CHAPTER 13: WHAT TO DO TO KEEP YOUR CREDIT HEALTH EXCELLENT

It is well and good to take care of negative items in your report that are dragging down your credit score. However, what is the point of doing this and then picking up fresh negative items?

Credit repair will take unnecessarily long to implement successfully if you do not overhaul your financial activity. Here are tips that will help you maintain the credit score increases that you worked so hard to achieve.

TIP #1: DRAW UP A BUDGET AND STICK TO IT

If there ever were a rule on keeping the credit on track and generally improving finance, it would read like this: *Live within your means.*

It may not always be the case, but in some case, you will find the need to take on a loan because some emergency or other came up. This is why, no matter how effective you are at making your paycheck stretch out over a month, you should save some money every month so that you do not have to take out credit so frequently, damaging your credit in the process.

Be responsible with your credit card. If you are a typical American with a penchant for whipping out the credit card, it is very likely that your card is the major reason behind your poor credit. Avoid making unnecessary purchases with frequency because you get closer to having your card maxed out this way.

Check your account every evening before you go to bed so you have an idea how your finances are faring. By and by, and with responsible behavior, you will get closer to an excellent credit score.

TIP #2: PAY ALL YOUR BILLS ON TIME

By now, you know that a large portion of your credit score—35% to be specific—hinges on your payment history. Payment history is not truly emphatic on whether you actually made your payments so much as it is on how timely your payments were. Even one late payment can seriously hurt your credit.

Ensure you know how much you owe in bills each month, and make sure you pay every bill. Even better, why not have an automated system agreed with your bank that will see allowed amounts automatically channeled toward paying off respective bills?

TIP #3: GET YOUR SECURED CREDIT CARD AND USE IT RESPONSIBLY

We have already covered the secured credit card and all the benefits that come with one. Be responsible for this card. Remember that the deposit amount you put in also acts as your credit limit. Keep the debt to credit ratio at 30% or below. Otherwise, keep working on increasing the card's credit limit if you figure that you will need to take out larger amounts in the future.

BONUS SECTION: MORTGAGE APPLICATION AND POOR CREDIT SCORE

BONUS: A MINI-GUIDE ON MORTGAGE APPLICATION FOR THOSE WITH POOR CREDIT

You may be tired of parting with rental fees every month or it could be that you have decided that it is about time you bought a house and start building equity. Unfortunately, it is difficult to be an attractive prospect for home loans if your credit is bad. In fact, only people who have a minimum score of 750 are ideal home loan candidates—these fellows get the most competitive interest rates.

As such, if your credit repair strategy implementation has not gotten you out of your credit bog, you may have to deal with more than a few mortgage denials or absurdly high-interest rates on the mortgages you can find. Still, this does not mean that it is impossible to get a mortgage and a competitive one at that.

First, let us examine the challenges that come with purchasing a house on poor credit.

CHALLENGES OF BUYING YOUR HOME WHEN YOUR CREDIT SCORE IS POOR

If your credit score is lower than 750, which it most likely is, you may have to accept that the most competitive mortgage rates in the market are off the table for you. Try to see things from the lender's point of view: the fellow with the higher credit score obviously poses a lower risk—with regard to a foreclosure in the future—or defaulting on the loan.

It thus makes sense to make the most competitive rates exclusive to them. If your score is poor, the Mortgage Company views you as a risky loan prospect. You may have to pay higher interest rates if you do manage to get a mortgage.

WHAT ARE YOUR OPTIONS?

The first step is to find out where your credit stands. Is your credit merely average without being spectacular or is it outright awful?

If even after applying quick credit repair strategies, your score still cannot crack 650, then it is about time you start researching on the "home loans with poor credit" topic. There is some good news for you though. These days, there are multiple programs available for first-time homebuyers (think the likes of Federal Housing Administration (FHA) loans) or people who want to buy a home with underwhelming credit.

FHA loans are a godsend, especially seeing as a score of 580 will still see you eligible for a home loan, provided you can put up a 3.5% down payment on the home. You also do not have to have 2 years of employment under your belt to qualify for FHA loans, a stipulation that comes with most loans.

Consider the HOPE program as well. The program allows people with poor credit to be approved for a home loan with a 0% down payment outlay. It is a neat program; you will be able to build your credit as you make payments going forward.

Besides both FHA and HOPE programs, you can consider saving up for a bigger down payment (or opting for a smaller, cheaper home). When you can put up a bigger down payment, you will be able to borrow less, which may raise the chances of being eligible for a mortgage.

CONCLUSION

We have come to the end of the book. Thank you for reading and congratulations on reading until the end.

As this book so clearly outlines, you are not doomed to lugging around your poor credit. With astute measures and responsible financial behavior, you will be able to inject new life into your credit.

The idea is to combine responsible financial behavior with the implementation of credit repair strategies. If you are consistent with this combined approach, you will begin to see marked improvements in a short time.

It is also important to point out that credit repair is not as hectic as some people make it out to be. While professional services tend to bring a refined, progressive approach to credit repair, fixing your credit is something you can succeed at on your own, as this book has so clearly shown.

If you found the book valuable, can you recommend it to others? One way to do that is to post a review on Amazon.

Please leave a review for this book on Amazon!

Thank you and good luck!